The

Bare Bones of the story of

King John and Magna Carta

With a profile of rebel Northern baron Sir William de Mowbray

PART O

What is Magn

Who were the feudal barons?

Who were the barons associated with Magna Carta?

What had brought about the need for Magna Carta?

What happened next?

What did Magna Carta Say? (A summary)

PART TWO: Sir William de Mowbray

1066 the first Montbrays arrive in England

A change of name

Sir William de Mowbray; Sir William and King John

Some of Sir William's famous descendants

The Family of William the Conqueror
King of England and Duke of Normandy

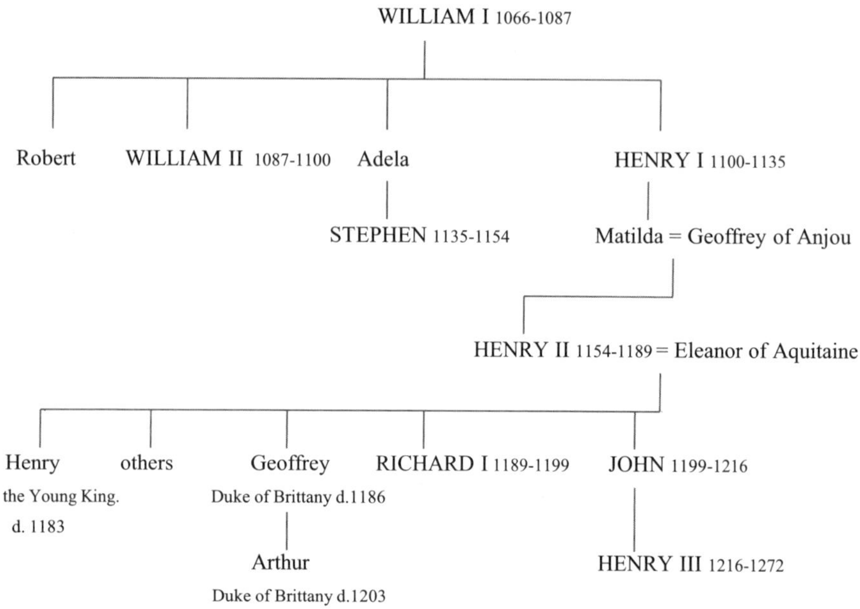

KING JOHN'S ANCESTORS

King John was a great-great-grandson of William the Conqueror, and since that king's death in 1087 there had not been a straightforward transfer of power. The Conqueror left Normandy to his eldest son, Duke Robert, and England to his middle son William, known as 'Rufus', leading to long-standing strife between the two brothers and a rebellion in England in favour of Robert. In 1100 William II met with a fatal 'accident' while hunting in the New Forest, enabling his younger brother Henry to claim the crown before Robert had the chance. Duke Robert's hopes of becoming King of England ended at the battle of Tinchebray in 1106 and he remained his brother's prisoner for the rest of his life.

King Henry I (1100-1135) had at least 29 children, only two of whom were legitimate, and when the son and heir drowned, the English barons were faced with the prospect of his sister Matilda becoming queen. Stephen of Blois, Matilda's cousin, seized the throne in 1135, setting in motion a drastic civil war that ended in a compromise whereby Stephen would remain king until his death and be succeeded by Matilda's son, Henry, Count of Anjou as Henry II. King Henry II's father was Geoffrey of Anjou, who wore a sprig of broom, *planta genista*, as his badge, which would become the name Plantagenet in later generations. In their own day Geoffrey and his children and grandchildren were known as the *Angevins*, the Men of Anjou, and were rumoured to be descended from Melusine, the beautiful daughter of Satan, hence their nickname the *Devil's Brood.*

KING JOHN AND MAGNA CARTA

What is Magna Carta?

*M*agna Carta, the 'Great Charter', is an 800-year-old document of approximately 3500 words written on parchment in a shorthand form of Latin. King John gave it his approval on 15 June 1215 in a meadow near Windsor called Runnymede in order to make peace with those of his barons who were in revolt. Of the copies made and sent to major towns and cities only four remain: two in the British Library in London, one in Salisbury Cathedral and one belonging to Lincoln Cathedral, but currently exhibited in Lincoln Castle. Not only did Magna Carta address the barons' grievances, it also contained clauses which protected the rights of the Church and ensured no freeman would suffer illegal imprisonment or be denied justice.

Within weeks of King John's death the following year, regents for his young son and successor issued a revised version in the hope of placating the still errant barons. There was another in 1217, and it was then that the term Magna Carta was first used in recognition of the unusually large size of the document, and in order to distinguish it from the shorter Charter of the Forest (Carta de Foresta) issued that November. Another version of 1225 eventually entered the statute book in 1297 during the reign of King John's grandson, Edward I.

Was Magna Carta a Success?

*I*n the immediate aftermath of June 1215, no, in that nothing came to fruition and civil war broke out within a few weeks. The fact also remains that despite the charter's enduring reputation as an icon of justice and liberty, the majority of the population, the unfree peasants, were not protected by its contents and remained in bondage to their immediate overlord, dependent on him for justice through his own manorial courts. Magna Carta has, however, maintained its unique symbolic status throughout the English-speaking world as an early attempt by subjects to force their king to curb his own power by accepting that not even the sovereign can be above the law. The charter, and in particular its successors, also limited the circumstances under which the king could raise money, and the 1225 revision was actually granted in return for a payment of tax.

What the barons concocted in 1215 as a weapon to be used against King John failed to do its job, but, adopted and adapted by his successors, it is seen as being the cornerstone of democracy in England. It has also formed the framework for systems of justice around the world, including the United States Bill of Rights (1791) the Universal Declaration of Human Rights (1948) and the European Convention on Human Rights (1950). Despite its unpretentious appearance, Magna Carta is still seen as a defence against tyranny, and the four survivors of 1215 remain amongst the most famous documents in the world.

800 years since the appearance of the original, only three clauses of its 1225 successor still remain on statute in the United Kingdom: the freedom of the English Church, the ancient liberties of the City of London (and other towns and ports), and a right to due legal process.

Who were the feudal barons?

The term 'baron' as used in the context of King John and the Magna Carta barons, was not a peerage title as it is today, but referred instead to any man who held his land directly from the king, that is, in the hierarchy of the feudal system he was a tenant-in-chief. The first generation of barons in England were Normans rewarded by William the Conqueror for their support at Hastings. Some of the barons did hold titles, however, Robert de Vere, earl of Oxford being one such example.

The baron was responsible for administration of the lands he held and in exchange for them would provide the king with knights and soldiers when needed, and/or pay a tax called 'shield money'. The barons then sub-let lands to others further down the feudal pyramid who would further sub-let, culminating with the peasants, who had nothing to offer in return except their unpaid labour. There were approximately 200 of these great land holders and in time there became a natural division into Greater and Lesser Barons as some became more powerful than others.

An individual parcel of land allotted by the king was called a *manor,* a word more readily associated today with large English country houses or French châteaux lying in acres of well-manicured grounds. A baron's land allocation as a whole was called an *Honour* and could be made up of dozens of manors.

Who were the barons associated with enforcing Magna Carta?

With his poor reputation and the lack of trust between the monarch and his subjects, it was feared King John would not abide by the 1215 agreement, so provision was included for the election of a committee of twenty-five barons to make sure he did. It was anticipated that these sureties would be elected in the near future, so neither their names nor their seals appear on the document. The barons' names subsequently associated with Magna Carta come from the *Chronica Majora,* an account compiled in the reign of Henry III by Matthew Paris, a monk of St Albans Abbey. However, Matthew was writing some years after the event, and relied heavily on his predecessor Roger of Wendover for his information. The list shows the Twenty-five were to be military men, drawn from the ranks of John's enemies, while moderates, or those remaining loyal to the king, such as the future Chief Justiciar, Hubert de Burgh, and William Marshal, earl of Pembroke were largely omitted.

THE TWENTY-FIVE SURETY BARONS

Richard de Clare, earl of Clare; William de Fors (or Fortibus), count of Aumale;

Geoffrey de Mandeville, earl of Gloucester; Saier de Quincy, earl of Winchester;

Henry de Bohun, earl of Hereford; Roger Bigod, earl of Norfolk;

Robert de Vere, earl of Oxford; William Marshal (Junior); Robert FitzWalter;

Gilbert de Clare; Eustace de Vesci; Hugh Bigod; William de Mowbray;

William de Lanvallei; Robert de Ros; Richard de Percy; John FitzRobert;

William Malet; Geoffrey de Say; John de Lacy, constable of Chester;

Roger de Montbegon (or Mumbezon); William de Huntingfield;

Richard de Munfichet (or Montfichet); William d'Aubigny (or d'Albini);

The Mayor of London (William Hardell)

de Mowbray

Fitzwalter

Malet

de Quincy

de Vesci

What brought about the need for Magna Carta?

Although eventually brought about by the barons' dissatisfaction with King John, Magna Carta was actually many years in gestation: the culmination of decades of problems in both England and Normandy. *The Devils Brood*, as the family of King Henry II (1154-1189) was popularly known, was frequently at war with itself, his sons fighting each other, rebelling against their father, and, on occasion, conspiring against him with their feisty mother, Eleanor of Aquitaïne. They were first and foremost Frenchmen, most of whom had been born there – although both King Richard I and his brother John were born at Oxford – who spoke French as their first language and viewed England as a detached outpost of their empire. In total, Henry II controlled about half of France, which he held as a tenant from his feudal overlord, first King Louis VII and later King Philip Augustus II. A tough soldier and competent administrator, he nevertheless had difficulty controlling his unruly vassals and opportunistic neighbours in his solid block of lands that stretched from the Scottish Borders to the Pyrenees.

In 1170, when he was 37, Henry II indicated he would begin delegating power to his sons. The eldest survivor, another Henry, then aged 16, was to be joint King of England, Duke of Normandy, Count of Anjou and Maine, who would reign with his father and be known as Henry the Young King. It was a terrible error of judgement resulting in an orgy of feuding and destruction lasting years. At the age of 18 the Young King, supported by his brothers Richard and Geoffrey, rebelled against his father, much to the delight of the King of France, who joined them. By 1183 Henry the Young King was 28, Richard 26, Geoffrey 25 and John 17, and the sons were in rebellion once again. When the Young King died of dysentery, the greed, jealousy and anger between the remaining brothers and their defiance of their father only deepened.

Geoffrey, the Duke of Brittany, was killed in a jousting accident in July 1186; three years later his father died a broken man after his remaining sons Richard, whom he had come truly to detest, and John, said to be his favourite, had transferred their allegiance to the King of France. Henry II was succeeded by Richard I, whom myth and legend have transformed into 'Lionheart', the perfect knight, a concept somewhat different from the disloyal, self-seeking son and bloodthirsty warrior as seen by some of his contemporaries.

So, before John had even come to the throne, the barons were already dispirited by the ongoing expense of the ruling family's struggles, and the lack of leadership from the absentee King Richard, who had hated England with a vengeance, spending only six months of his ten year reign here. They were also hugely disgruntled by the swingeing taxes levied to pay for Richard's crusading adventures in the Holy Land, and, to add insult to injury, when he fell into the hands of European enemies on his way back from the East, they had also to help raise the then staggering sum of £100,000 for the king's ransom. During his brother's incarceration, Prince John had allied with King Philip of France, and treacherously made some Norman castles over to him. Once released, Richard decided to raise another small fortune for building more castles, another enormous financial burden for both Normandy and England. King Richard I died of an infected wound in 1199 and left no legitimate children.

Letter from the aged Eleanor of Aquitaine to Pope Celestine in 1193 asking him to secure Richard's release

... I am wasted away by sorrow ... My guts are torn from me... The young king and the count of Brittany sleep in dust. Two sons ... survive to punish me... King Richard is held in chains. His brother, John, depletes his [i.e. Richard's] *kingdom with iron* [sword] *and lays it waste with fire... Death is my wish, my life is loathsome...*

Thus, at the age 31 John, once nicknamed 'Lackland', became King of England and master of vast areas of France, but the reign started badly. In 1200 he put away his first wife and married Isabella of Angoulême, the barely thirteen-year-old fiancée of one his leading vassals in Aquitaine. King Philip II, John's overlord, commanded him to make amends, and when he disobeyed and refused to appear before him it gave Philip the golden opportunity to take away many of his French territories and bestow some of them on John's young nephew, Arthur of Brittany, son of his late brother Geoffrey, whom many saw as the rightful successor to Richard I. Arthur disappeared in 1203 while imprisoned by his uncle, rumoured murdered by him. This, and John's appalling treatment of noble prisoners who had supported his nephew, turned his already disaffected Norman vassals against him even more, and when the city of Rouen surrendered to the besieging forces of King Philip in June 1204, it marked the end of John's rule in Normandy.

In some ways this loss of continental lands was a good thing for England, in that the king and barons' full attention henceforth could be focused upon it, encouraging a separate English identity to develop. However, King John saw things differently and, confident he could reverse the setback, began what was to be ten years of wringing money out of his remaining subjects in England and Ireland, thinking nothing of selling justice and terrifying his debtors. There were also several new taxes, including what today would be seen as an income tax. John was already noted for his severity, but driving his vassal William de Braose from his Irish lands in 1210 for non-payment of a debt, and then starving his wife and son to death at Windsor, was a significant nail in his coffin as far as many of his barons were concerned.

In 1207 John fell out with Pope Innocent III over the choice of a new Archbishop of Canterbury, so England was placed under Papal Interdict, meaning clergy could not take services and nobody could be married in church or buried in consecrated ground. John responded by pillaging treasures from churches and monasteries, imposing heavy fines on the clergy, even imprisoning them, acts for which he was excommunicated in 1209. The chroniclers, the nearest equivalent of today's newspaper reporters, and on whom historians must largely depend for descriptions of the nature and behaviour of individuals, were monks, so obviously many were biased in their accounts, helping accelerate the decline in King John's already shaky reputation. This, together with his apparent lack of fear of the pope must have revitalised the old superstition that John's Angevin ancestors truly were the Devil's Brood. He made peace with Innocent in 1212, finally accepting his candidate Stephen Langton as Archbishop of Canterbury, and made partial restitution for what he had taken from the Church. Henceforth, Pope Innocent would be John's supporter against his increasingly rebellious barons, but it would come at too high a price, for on 21 April 1214, John accepted the pope as feudal overlord of England.

By 1214 the king had accumulated vast resources, spent a fortune buying support on the continent and was planning a massive assault against France, for which he had been levying the *scutage* or 'shield money' tax at such exorbitant rates and more frequently than ever previously known. Some barons had few or no interests in Normandy, so whether John reclaimed it or not was largely irrelevant to them and hardly worth the effort or expense. In July 1214 his hopes were ended and his war chest melted away when his allies lost the battle of Bouvines in Flanders, and when the king returned and faced his English barons the following autumn it was obvious there would be serious conflict ahead, possibly even civil war.

The next few months saw rebel barons, mainly based in the north and east of England, rallying support. King John had agreed to a meeting on 5 May 1215 at Northampton, but when he failed to appear the rebels renounced their feudal ties, and appointed as their leader Robert Fitzwalter, who adopted the name 'Marshal of the Army of God and the Holy Church'. They took control of Lincoln and Exeter, and once the city of London had welcomed them twelve days later they were joined by other, more moderate, barons who had been biding their time. On 10 June the rebel leaders presented their draft demands for reform. Known now as the *Articles of the Barons*, this remarkable document still exists and may be seen at the British Library. Over the next few days, under the guidance and mediation of Stephen Langton, these demands were redrafted to produce the document presented to King John on 15 June.

What happened next?

A few days after John had put his seal to the document the barons renewed their oaths of allegiance. He was, however, merely buying time, and within weeks, possibly before the committee of 25 surety barons could be appointed, he reneged on his promise, aided and abetted by Pope Innocent. The barons still controlled London, which they refused to surrender until John complied with the new charter, so the pope issued a papal bull (also kept now in the British Library) nullifying it and decrying its proposals as being illegal, base and shameful; Archbishop Stephen Langton was suspended from duties for his part in formulating it.

The heavy-handed 'security clauses' made the 1215 charter unworkable. It was inconceivable that John could continue to function as ruler when, if he or any of his officials had transgressed and he had not made redress within 40 days:

> ... *the four barons* [to whom the complaint against him had been made] *shall refer the matter to the rest of the twenty-five barons, who may distrain upon and assail us in every way possible, with the support of the whole community of the land, by seizing our castles, lands, possessions, or anything else saving only our own person and those of the queen and our children...*

Civil war broke out in September 1215, with some of the barons breaking their oath of allegiance and offering the throne of England to Prince Louis, son of Philip of France. Hostilities continued until 18 October 1216, when King John died at Newark Castle in Nottinghamshire, probably of dysentery. In November a revised version of Magna Carta was issued by William Marshal, regent for the new king, nine-year-old Henry III, in order to regain the barons' support, but some, backed by French soldiers and mercenaries already in the country, chose to continue with the plan to install the French prince. The bitter conflict continued until September 1217, resulting in a victory for Henry III.

WHAT DID MAGNA CARTA SAY? (SUMMARY)

The document was not divided into separate clauses: the numbering system used today was introduced in 1759 by judge and politician Sir William Blackstone. (The clauses below in bold and marked with ++ are still on statute in the United Kingdom. In the original, 39 & 40 are not separated). The Great Charta begins with King John's titles, although by this time much of this was wishful thinking on his part:

JOHN, by the grace of God King of England, Lord of Ireland, Duke of Normandy and Aquitaine, and Count of Anjou, to his archbishops, bishops, abbots, earls, barons, justices, foresters, sheriffs, stewards, servants, and to all his officials and loyal subjects, Greeting...

There follows a list of the leading persons who advised the king, all male and including the bishops, the Master of the Knights Templar in England, William Marshal and Hubert de Burgh.

++ (1) FIRST, THAT WE HAVE GRANTED TO GOD, and by this present charter have confirmed for us and our heirs in perpetuity, that the English Church shall be free, and shall have its rights undiminished, and its liberties unimpaired. ....TO ALL FREE MEN OF OUR KINGDOM we have also granted, for us and our heirs for ever, all the liberties written out below, to have and to keep for them and their heirs, of us and our heirs.

(Clauses 2-11): mainly rules and conditions concerned with the holding and inheriting of lands, including rules relating to widows of land holders and their remarriages; dealing with debts; dealing with money borrowed from Jews.

(12) No 'scutage' or 'aid' may be levied in our kingdom without its general consent, unless it is for the ransom of our person, to make our eldest son a knight, and (once) to marry our eldest daughter. For these purposes only a reasonable 'aid' may be levied. 'Aids' from the city of London are to be treated similarly.

++ (13) The city of London shall enjoy all its ancient liberties and free customs, both by land and by water. We also will and grant that all other cities, boroughs, towns, and ports shall enjoy all their liberties and free customs.

(Clauses 14-26): forms of 'aid' not covered by clause 12; lawsuits and fines.

(Clauses 27-37): protection of rights including property; payment of dues for goods; fair trial; weights and measures to be standardised throughout the kingdom.

(38) In future no official shall place a man on trial upon his own unsupported statement, without producing credible witnesses to the truth of it.

++ (39) No free man shall be seized or imprisoned, or stripped of his rights or possessions, or outlawed or exiled, or deprived of his standing in any way, nor will we proceed with force against him, or send others to do so, except by the lawful judgment of his equals or by the law of the land.

(40) ***To no one will we sell, to no one deny or delay right or justice.***

(Clauses 41-51): various including safe conduct of merchants and others in and out of the country; clauses referring specifically to the forests; promise to remove from office the kinsmen of Gerard de Athée, a much-hated mercenary employed by John to control parts of Wales; removal of foreign knights and mercenaries.

(Clauses 52-59): putting right wrongs regarding the taking of property and goods by the Crown (including previous monarchs) and the imposition of unjust fines (the 25 barons and the Archbishop of Canterbury to be the judges in these matters); similarly the Welsh to have a just hearing; the return of Welsh and Scottish hostages.

(60) All these customs and liberties that we have granted shall be observed in our kingdom in so far as concerns our own relations with our subjects. Let all men of our kingdom, whether clergy or laymen, observe them similarly in their relations with their own men.

THE SECURITY CLAUSES – THE 25 BARONS

(61) SINCE WE HAVE GRANTED ALL THESE THINGS for God, for the better ordering of our kingdom, and to allay the discord that has arisen between us and our barons, and since we desire that they shall be enjoyed in their entirety, with lasting strength, for ever, we give and grant to the barons the following security:

The barons shall elect twenty-five of their number to keep, and cause to be observed with all their might, the peace and liberties granted and confirmed to them by this charter.

If we, our chief justice, our officials, or any of our servants offend in any respect against any man, or transgress any of the articles of the peace or of this security, and the offence is made known to four of the said twenty-five barons, they shall come to us - or in our absence from the kingdom to the chief justice - to declare it and claim immediate redress. If we, or in our absence abroad the chief justice, make no redress within forty days, reckoning from the day on which the offence was declared to us or to him, the four barons shall refer the matter to the rest of the twenty-five barons, who may distrain upon and assail us in every way possible, with the support of the whole community of the land, by seizing our castles, lands, possessions, or anything else saving only our own person and those of the queen and our children, until they have secured such redress as they have determined upon. Having secured the redress, they may then resume their normal obedience to us.

Any man who so desires may take an oath to obey the commands of the twenty-five barons for the achievement of these ends, and to join with them in assailing us to the utmost of his power. We give public and free permission to take this oath to any man who so desires, and at no time will we prohibit any man from taking it. Indeed, we will compel any of our subjects who are unwilling to take it to swear it at our command.

If one of the twenty-five barons dies or leaves the country, or is prevented in any other way from discharging his duties, the rest of them shall choose another baron in his place, at their discretion, who shall be duly sworn in as they were.

In the event of disagreement among the twenty-five barons on any matter referred to them for decision, the verdict of the majority present shall have the same validity as a unanimous verdict of the whole twenty-five, whether these were all present or some of those summoned were unwilling or unable to appear.

The twenty-five barons shall swear to obey all the above articles faithfully, and shall cause them to be obeyed by others to the best of their power.

We will not seek to procure from anyone, either by our own efforts or those of a third party, anything by which any part of these concessions or liberties might be revoked or diminished. Should such a thing be procured, it shall be null and void and we will at no time make use of it, either ourselves or through a third party.

(62) We have remitted and pardoned fully to all men any ill-will, hurt, or grudges that have arisen between us and our subjects, whether clergy or laymen, since the beginning of the dispute. We have in addition remitted fully, and for our own part have also pardoned, to all clergy and laymen any offences committed as a result of the said dispute between Easter in the sixteenth year of our reign [i.e. 1215] and the restoration of peace.

In addition we have caused letters patent to be made for the barons, bearing witness to this security and to the concessions set out above, over the seals of Stephen archbishop of Canterbury, Henry archbishop of Dublin, the other bishops named above, and Master Pandulf [the papal representative].

(63) *IT IS ACCORDINGLY OUR WISH AND COMMAND that the English Church shall be free, and that men in our kingdom shall have and keep all these liberties, rights, and concessions, well and peaceably in their fullness and entirety for them and their heirs, of us and our heirs, in all things and all places for ever.*

Both we and the barons have sworn that all this shall be observed in good faith and without deceit. Witness the abovementioned people and many others.

Given by our hand in the meadow that is called Runnymede, between Windsor and Staines, on the fifteenth day of June in the seventeenth year of our reign

The full text can be found at: http://www.bl.uk/magna-carta/articles/magna-carta-english-translation#sthash.Ab498WC4.dpuf

"... the greatest constitutional document of all times – the foundation of the freedom of the individual against the arbitrary authority of the despot."

Lord Denning (1899-1999), Judge and Master of the Rolls, speaking of Magna Carta in 1965

"Magna Carta is not primarily significant for what it was, but rather for what it was made to be."

Erwin Griswold (1904-1994), Dean of Harvard Law School and Solicitor General of the United States

Henry II and his children from an early fourteenth century family tree. From left: William (died young); Henry the Young King; King Richard I; Matilda, Duchess of Saxony; Geoffrey of Brittany; Eleanor, Queen of Castile; Joan, Queen of Sicily; King John (British Library Royal MS 14 B VI)

A 1215 copy of Magna Carta - the only surviving copy in landscape format - given to collector Sir Robert Cotton in 1629; according to one account it had been found in a London tailor's shop (British Library Cotton MS Augustus II.106)

The Battle of Lincoln 2017, defending the castle; Matthew Paris *Chronica Majora* (Cambridge, Parker MS 16, fol. 51v)

Lincoln Castle 800 years later (photo licensed under the Creative Commons Attribution 2.0 Generic licence, Karen Roe)

St Andrew's Church, Epworth with, below left, a Mowbray shield carving in the north porch; Samuel Wesley, father of John and Charles, was rector here in the eighteenth century and is buried in the churchyard. The Mowbrays' manor house lay on the piece of land on the right of the picture known today as *Vinegarth,* where the floor tile below right was discovered during excavations in the 1970's. (© St Andrew's/M. Roberts)

The Mowbray lion; clockwise from top left: Haxey village green, North Lincolnshire; Holy Trinity Church, Goodramgate, York; Holy Trinity Church, Long Melford, Suffolk; St Mary's Church, Melton Mowbray, Leicestershire; The Mowbray Arms public house, Epworth, North Lincolnshire; St James's Church, High Melton, South Yorkshire © Various

Was the Charter of Liberties of King John (Magna Carta) a new concept in 1215?

No: it bears remarkable similarities to the much shorter *Charter of Liberties of Henry I*, King John's great-grandfather, whose 'Coronation Charter' was an attempt to right the wrongs of William II and make himself a more attractive option to the English barons than his brother Robert. This charter was clearly a source of ideas in 1215; until then the ruler had imposed the rules on his subjects, but under Magna Carta the roles were reversed.

Others include:

Charter of Liberties of King Stephen, 1136

The Treaty of Westminster (Stephen), 1154

Charter of Liberties of Henry II, 1154

The Constitutions of Clarendon (Henry II), 1164

The Assize of Clarendon (Henry II), 1166

In the reign of King John's son the most radical charters, which limited the monarch's power and sowed the seed of the parliamentary system, were:

The Provisions of Oxford 1258

The Provisions of Westminster 1260

The Statute of Marlborough 1267: these 29 Marlborough laws went on the Statute Book long before anything from the 1225 version of Magna Carta was finally made law in 1297. Four still remain, but at the time of writing – January 2015 – discussions are underway to have two of them, dealing with debt-collection, repealed as obsolete, having been replaced by new laws in March 2014.

"We all know that Magna Carta was actually about one group of privileged and powerful people protecting themselves from someone who was even more privileged and powerful. But it has become something else."

Neil MacGregor, Director of the British Museum

The City of Lincoln and Magna Carta

As one of the most important cities in King John's realm, Lincoln received a copy of the Great Charter of 1215, one of only four known to have survived, and the only one to have an inscription on the back – "Lincoln". Lincoln Castle is the only place in the world to exhibit a 1215 Magna Carta and a 1217 Carta de Foresta together.

On 4th July 1940, the Independence Day holiday, a long queue at the World Fair in New York was waiting to see the Lincoln Magna Carta in the British Pavilion. An electrician in the control room spotted an unfamiliar overnight bag: it was ticking. He and his boss then carried the bag through the crowded Pavilion in search of the head of security, who was engaged in guarding Magna Carta itself. He carried the bag outside. Two officers of the New York Police Department Bomb and Forgery Squad, Freddy Socha and Joe Lynch, picked it up, carried it to open ground and were cutting the bag open when the bomb exploded killing both of them instantly and seriously injuring two of their colleagues. A massive investigation followed but the case remains unsolved and the $26,000 reward is still unclaimed. (*http://www.bloomberg.com/news/articles/2010-06-25*)

By the time the World Fair closed in October, Britain was at the mercy of German bombers and it was decided the journey back home for the document would be too risky, so the Lincoln Magna Carta spent much of the Second World War at Fort Knox in Kentucky, where it remained until 1947. Winston Churchill was believed to be toying with the idea of giving it to the United States in the hope the Americans would take up arms on our side, but could hardly have expected Lincoln Cathedral to let it go for good. (*http://www.lincolnshireecho.co.uk/Flashback-Winston-Churchill-s-secret-plot-Lincoln*)

"Here is a law which is above the King and which even he must not break. This reaffirmation of a supreme law and its expression in a general charter is the great work of Magna Carta; and this alone justifies the respect in which men have held it"

Sir Winston Churchill

SIR WILLIAM DE MOWBRAY

1066 and the first Montbrays arrive in England

The first Mowbrays to be found on record as having associations with England are Geoffrey de Montbray (or Montbrai), bishop of Coutances in Normandy, his brother Roger and Roger's son Robert. The family's *caput,* or chief manor, was the village of Montbray in Normandy, hence the family name now more familiar as 'Mowbray'. A younger son, expecting to inherit very little, Geoffrey first became a soldier before taking up a lucrative career in the Church and was present at the Battle of Hastings. A great friend of William the Conqueror, he officiated at his coronation in Westminster Abbey on December 25 1066 and again at his funeral in Caen in 1087, when the putrefying corpse exploded with great force and emitted such evil odours that several of those gathered in the cathedral ran outside gasping for fresh air. Geoffrey was a useful sort of chap to have around, equally at home singing Mass before a battle or ordering bodily mutilations of those who presented a threat to his king and benefactor, so it is hardly surprising that he became one of the Conqueror's tenants-in-chief and consequently one of the ten richest men in England.

Less is known of his elder brother Roger, possibly killed at Hastings, but Roger's son Robert, a fearsome and lawless character made earl of Northumberland by William I, was Geoffrey's frequent companion. It is probable that Robert de Mowbray built the early wooden castle in Yorkshire around which the town of Thirsk developed, and the Vale of Mowbray was named after him. After the friendship and patronage they had enjoyed under the feudal system of the Conqueror, the uncle and nephew felt less secure under the rule of his son, William II, and rebelled. Many involved in that uprising suffered terrible executions or mutilations, but somehow both the bishop and the earl escaped persecution. Wisely, Bishop Geoffrey retired to Coutances, where he died in 1093, but Robert rebelled again, for which he spent the last thirty years of his life in prison, mostly at Windsor. His collection of manors in both Normandy and England was broken up and redistributed to other feudal barons, his marriage annulled, and his wife married off to someone else long before he died in 1129.

A change of name: the 'new' Mowbrays

Magna Carta baron Sir William de Mowbray's grandfather was Roger de Mowbray, founder of the family that would eventually become dukes of Norfolk, but there appears to be little connection to the two original Mowbray barons, as Roger had not even been a Mowbray by birth, nor had some of his extensive lands in England any connection to them.

St Martin d'Aubigny was a village a few miles from Montbray, and, just as their neighbours had done, the feudal lords of the manor took their own *caput,* as their family name. In 1106 Nigel d'Aubigny, a younger son, had a very large number of manors in England and a handful in Normandy conveyed to him by King Henry I for services rendered, which upon Nigel's death in 1129 went to his young son Roger d'Aubigny. Surviving documents reveal that Henry I wanted the boy to be known as Roger de Mowbray (the spelling varies and also appeared as Montbray, Molbrai and Moubrai) and scholars are not agreed as to why.

There is a possibility that Nigel d'Aubigny's mother was Amicia de Montbray (Mowbray), aunt of Robert earl of Northumberland imprisoned at Windsor, which would make Nigel and Robert first cousins, but this is not proven. The scenario is further complicated, however, by Nigel having married Maud de Laigle, formerly wife of the imprisoned Robert, but later Nigel had their union annulled and Roger was not Maud's son. A more plausible explanation is that, although several of Roger's English manors would be larger and more productive than Montbray, a Norman possession at this time would still hold superior status over English manors and give its name to the Honour, so it would follow that Roger would be Roger of Montbray.

The 'new' Mowbray family's holdings were at their peak in the time of Roger's father Nigel, always a staunch 'king's man' who did not put a foot wrong, whereas his son was forced to surrender some of his manors for committing several misdemeanours, including rebelling against Henry II in favour of the Young King. It was at this time, 1176, that the Mowbray defensive wooden castles at Thirsk and Kirby Malzeard in Yorkshire and Kinard (now Owston) Ferry in Lincolnshire were destroyed on the king's orders and never rebuilt.

Sir Roger was one of the most generous of his family in the founding or endowing religious houses, including Byland Abbey in Yorkshire where extensive and beautiful ruins still bear testimony to his great wealth. He also founded a very important leper hospital at Burton Lazars about a-mile-and-a-half away from Melton Mowbray, both of which were among his allocation of Leicestershire manors.

Roger had a long and exciting life and went on crusade in both his thirties and sixties. On his last foray to the exotic East he was captured by Saladin and ransomed by the Knights Templar, but died in the Holy Land in 1188 and was buried in or near the modern city of Tyre in Lebanon. A later tradition, probably concocted by monks at Newburgh Priory, another of his religious foundations, claims he came back to Yorkshire accompanied by a faithful lion he had rescued from the jaws of a vicious dragon on his long trek home across Europe. His son Nigel de Mowbray succeeded him but died in the Holy Land less than three years later, and was in turn succeeded by his son William, aged about fifteen.

THE HONOUR of MOWBRAY c.1170

The Honour was one of the largest of all with a total in excess of 250 manors, although this would vary over the years as some would be forfeited by a particular baron for various transgressions, or new ones bestowed upon him for special services rendered, while others might be acquired through marriage. This particular Honour in 1170, before Sir Roger de Mowbray lost three castles for having rebelled against Henry II, comprised roughly:

NORMANDY: 20 manors, including Montbray (the head, or chief manor – the *caput*); 3 castles.

LINCOLNSHIRE: 25, including the cluster in the Isle of Axholme around Epworth, seen by some historians as the most important of the whole honour, kept as *demesne* lands, that is, for the baron's own use and not sub-let; one castle, at Kinard (Owston) Ferry.

NOTTINGHAMSHIRE: 11

LEICESTERSHIRE: 22, including Melton Mowbray, Burton Lazars (site of Sir Roger's leper hospital) and Thorpe Arnold (kept as *demesne*)

WARWICKSHIRE & NORTHAMPTONSHIRE: 34, including Brinklow with a castle.

YORKSHIRE: in excess of 160 including the castles of Kirby Malzeard, Thirsk and Burton-in-Lonsdale; *demesne* lands were at Hovingham, Galphay, Grewelthorpe, Winksley, Laverton and Braithwaite.

(For details of the manors and contemporary documentation relating to them see the exhaustive research of Diana Greenway in *Charters of the Honour of Mowbray,* OUP 1972. For a full list see Marilyn Roberts, *The Mowbray Legacy,* 2012.)

The Mowbray Family 1066-1481

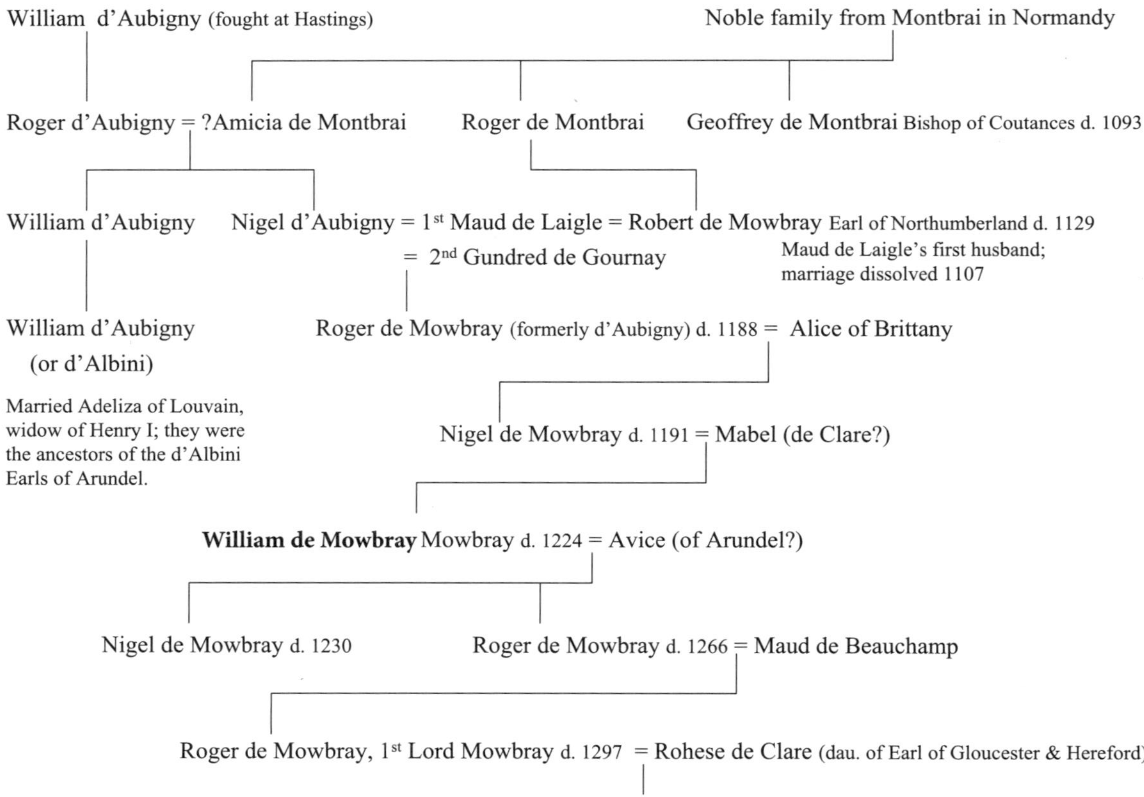

John de Mowbray, 2nd Lord Mowbray hanged at York, 1322 = Alina de Braose (dau. of Ld. of Bramber & Gower)

John de Mowbray, 3rd Lord Mowbray 1310-1361 = Joan Plantagenet (great-granddaughter of Henry III)

John de Mowbray, 4th Lord Mowbray 1340-1368 = Elizabeth Segrave (great-granddaughter of Edward I)

John de Mowbray d. 1383
Earl of Nottingham

Thomas Mowbray 1st Duke of Norfolk = Elizabeth Fitzalan (dau. of 11th Earl of Arundel)
b. 1366, d. in exile in Venice, 1399

Thomas Mowbray
E. of Nottingham
beheaded 1405,
aged 19

John Mowbray = Katherine Neville
1392-1432 dau. of E. of Westmorland
2nd Duke of Norfolk

Margaret Mowbray
= Sir Robert Howard

Isabel Mowbray
= 1st Henry Ferrers
= 2nd James Berkeley

John Mowbray 1415-1461 3rd Duke of Norfolk = Eleanor Bourchier
(gr-dau of Thomas of Woodstock)

John Mowbray 1444-1476 4th Duke of Norfolk = Elizabeth Talbot (dau. of E. of Shrewsbury)
The Mowbray dukedom extinct, 1476

Lady Anne Mowbray 1472-1481, Countess of Norfolk = Richard Duke of York, son of Edward IV
later one of the Princes in the Tower

Sir William de Mowbray

*A*s Sir Roger's grandson, Sir William de Mowbray was one of the great northern barons who also held land in Normandy, but the bulk of his income came from Lincolnshire, Nottinghamshire, Leicestershire, Northamptonshire, Warwickshire and Yorkshire. The Honour of Mowbray was one of the largest of all, comprising in excess of 250 manors in 1170.

The lands a baronial family reserved for its own needs and did not sub-let were known as *demesne* and in Mowbray's case included a very productive cluster from among his Lincolnshire holdings: the manors of Epworth, Belton, Beltoft, Belwood, Butterwick, Burnham, Melwood, Haxey and Kinard (now Owston) Ferry in the area still known as the Isle of Axholme, which scholars have claimed were the most productive of the whole Honour. From among his dozens of Yorkshire manors he reserved Thirsk, Hovingham and a cluster in the vicinity of Kirby Malzeard for his own needs. Three castles had been destroyed, but William still held those at Montbray, Burton-in-Lonsdale in Yorkshire and Brinklow in Warwickshire.

Unlike castles, manor houses, although sometimes fortified, were more comfortable, residential properties. The Mowbray manor house at Epworth lay beside St Andrew's Church and remains of it were discovered in the 1970's. Sir William de Mowbray was a powerful and extremely wealthy man, able to deal in vast sums of money. His fine households at Epworth and other parts of the country would be run along the same lines as that of the king, with officers such as stewards, constables of the stables and clerks to deal with the paperwork, together with butlers and a multitude of lesser household servants and labourers to tend to his every whim and need.

In the thirteenth century *Histoire des Ducs de Normandie et des Rois d'Angleterre* he is described as being 'as small as a dwarf, but very generous and valiant', but since this book was compiled from various earlier chronicles we have no guarantee of the veracity of the description. Sir William was among those held hostage with King Richard I in the early 1190's and paid at least £100 as his share of the king's ransom, a vast amount in those days, not long after he had paid the same amount for the relief, or transfer, of his late father's lands, having reached the age at which he could claim control over them. From knowing his whereabouts at certain dates we can see that he was involved in most major events of King John's reign.

*U*pon King Richard's death in 1199, Mowbray, with the other barons, Greater and Lesser, swore fealty (loyalty) to his brother John, on the assurance that each would have his rights, but he, like many others, fortified his strongholds in case of trouble; he was abroad in the King's service in 1202 and again in 1203. When King John lost the Norman possessions in 1204 William's lands in Normandy were gone forever. He went with John on expedition to Ireland in 1210, but soon afterwards was sufficiently concerned about the way things were going to strengthen his properties yet again.

It is hardly surprising that Sir William de Mowbray sided with those barons who revolted against King John in 1215, since he had a long-standing grudge against him that went back almost to the beginning of the reign. Only twenty-five years earlier, Sir William's grandfather had reached agreement with the Stuteville family over lands of theirs that had, perhaps not entirely legally, been awarded to Nigel d'Aubigny by Henry I, so when the case was brought up again by William de Stuteville in 1200, King John could have made a final and fair ruling. John was, however, notorious for extortion and the accepting of bribes, so William de Mowbray hoped a 'gift' to him of 2000 marks (about £1,333) would help win his case. This was at a time when the income of even the most affluent baron would not exceed £800 a year, so at today's rates it would represent an eye-wateringly large amount of money. Mowbray met Stuteville, who apparently had made a similar 'gift' to the King, at the Bishop of Lincoln's country house at Louth in January 1201 for the judgement, which resulted in an unsatisfactory compromise: an expensive lesson for both parties. There is a disturbing irony about the fact that Mowbray, who himself had been prepared to buy justice through the means of a massive bribe, was to be one of the select band responsible in 1215 for ensuring that such practices henceforth would be illegal.

When King John died in 1216 the reason for the unrest should have died with him, and many barons were willing to make a fresh start and accept the child Henry III, John's young son, as their king. William de Mowbray, however, and other like-minded barons continued to give their support to Louis of France in preference. The unfortunate inhabitants of Lincoln suffered terribly as a consequence of the two sides doing battle there in May 1217, and we are indebted to the chronicler Roger of Wendover for an account of the hardships, including the poverty of the French soldiers and the havoc and misery they brought to the ordinary people as they moved around the country:

They therefore marched through the valley of Belvoir, and there everything fell into the hands of these robbers, because the soldiers of the French kingdom, being as it were the refuse and scum of that country, left nothing at all untouched, and their poverty and wretchedness was so great that they had not enough bodily clothing to cover their nakedness.

When royal reinforcements led by the regent William Marshal arrived Mowbray and his comrades scoffed at their scouts' estimates of their numbers:

The barons who were in the city and the French felt such great confidence of success in their cause, that when their messengers told them of the approach of their adversaries they only *laughed at them, and continued to hurl missiles from their mangonels, to destroy the walls of the castle.*

They were deceived, and the relieving troops were able to enter the city fairly easily and engage those attacking the castle:

Then sparks of fire were seen to dart, and sounds of dreadful thunder were heard to burst forth from the blows of swords against helmeted heads; but at length, by means of the crossbowmen, by whose skill the horses of the barons were mown down and killed like pigs, the party of the barons was greatly weakened, for, when the horses fell to the earth slain, their riders were taken prisoners, as there was no one to rescue them. Had it not been for the effect of relationship and blood, not a single one of all of them would have escaped. ...There were also made prisoners, the barons Robert Fitzwalter, Richard de Montfitchet, William de Mowbray...

The city of Lincoln was subjected to such looting by the victorious soldiers who, it was claimed carried off great heaps of goods as though coming home from a fair, that the battle gained the nickname of the 'Battle of Lincoln Fair'. Many English men and women must have thought the reign of the new king was even worse than that of his father. To avoid what Roger of Wendover quaintly describes as 'insult' many women took to the River Witham in boats and hundreds drowned. The pope's representative justified the action and the pillaging of churches and even the cathedral treasures by Henry III's soldiers as acceptable since the rebel barons had been excommunicated men. Roger of Wendover, a monk, tried to justify the carnage against the ordinary people:

> *It must be believed that this defeat happened to Louis and the barons of England as a just dispensation from God, for as they had now continued nearly two years under sentence of excommunication, unless they were corrected by divine punishment, men would say 'there is no God' and so there would be none who acted rightly, no, not one.*

By the autumn of 1217 the conflict was over, with Henry III recognised as rightful king and the retreating mercenaries and French trying to reach the south coast having to run the gauntlet of the villages they had terrorised earlier. Not long afterwards Mowbray was ransomed by Hubert de Burgh, part of the deal being that he would surrender to Hubert his manor of Banstead in Surrey that had come to the family through his mother. In 1223 the king again took away some of his lands when he defaulted in his service against the Welsh, but they were restored before the end of the year, whereas Banstead was never in the Mowbrays' possession again.

Sir William had married a noble lady named Avice, possibly a relative from the Arundel branch of the d'Aubigny family, and died in March 1224 at his house in Epworth. He was buried at Newburgh Priory in Yorkshire and succeeded by his sons Nigel, who died in 1230 leaving no heir, and then Roger, still a child, who was Nigel's successor. This Roger's son, also named Roger, was one of those called to the Model Parliament of Edward I in 1295, and thus became the first Lord Mowbray. (Sir William's brother Philip was the founder of the Scottish Mowbrays, while another brother, Robert, was the founder of the Mowbrays of Kirklington in Yorkshire.)

A few of Sir William's descendants

The modern surnames Daubeney and Dabney derive from d'Aubigny, while Mowbray itself is not common today, although there are still pockets of both names around the country.

The dynasty died out in 1481 with the death of Sir William's several times great-granddaughter, Lady Anne Mowbray, daughter of the fourth and last Mowbray duke of Norfolk. At the time of her marriage to Prince Richard of York, younger son of King Edward IV, she was only five and the prince four years of age. She died three weeks before her ninth birthday and had the distinction of being the only member of the Mowbray family to be buried in

Westminster Abbey. Anne's coffin was found two miles away on a London building site in December 1964. Her husband, the younger of the Princes in the Tower, disappeared in 1483, the same year that King Richard III divided the Mowbray inheritance between Anne's heirs, her elderly kinsmen Lord John Howard, who became Duke of Norfolk in a new creation, and Lord William Berkeley, made Earl of Nottingham.

A few of Sir William de Mowbray's more famous descendants include: Thomas Mowbray, first duke of Norfolk, born at Epworth around 1366, and who appears in Shakespeare's *King Richard II*; the cousins Katherine Howard and Anne Boleyn, executed queens of Henry VIII; Anne Boleyn's daughter, Queen Elizabeth I; Lady Jane Grey; U.S. Presidents George Washington, Thomas Jefferson and George W. Bush; Lady Diana Spencer, Princess of Wales; Sarah Ferguson, Duchess of York; actors Audrey Hepburn, Olivia de Havilland and her sister Joan Fontaine; the writer C S Lewis; HM Queen Elizabeth II.

FURTHER READING – A SHORT SELECTION

(The books by J. C. Holt and W. L. Warren remain the classic studies of King John and his reign)

Breay, Claire *Magna Carta: Manuscripts and Myths* British Library 2002

Carpenter, Prof. David *Magna Carta* Penguin Classics 2015

Holt, J. C. *Magna Carta*, 2nd ed. Cambridge University Press 1992

Holt, J. C., *the Northerners: A Study in the Reign of King John* Oxford University Press 1961

Roberts, Marilyn *The Mowbray Legacy* Queens-Haven Publications 2nd ed. 2012

Warren, W. L. *Henry II* Eyre Methuen 1973

Warren, W. L. *King John* Eyre & Spottiswoode 1961

All of the above carry extensive bibliographies.